The

WEDDING

GODFATHER

ADVICE YOU CAN'T REFUSE

by JOHN GOOLSBY

GODFATHER 🌹 PUBLISHING

GODFATHER PUBLISHING

This softcover edition was printed in 2012 by Godfather Publishing

THE WEDDING GODFATHER, ADVICE YOU CAN'T REFUSE.

ISBN
PAPERBACK - 978-0-9883755-0-5
KINDLE - 978-0-9883755-1-2
EPUB - 978-0-9883755-2-9

FIRST GODFATHER PUBLISHING EDITION PUBLISHED 2012

Cover & Book design by Ian Berg
Editing by Alan and Carole Berg & Jodi Bruskin

Thank you to my team of expert filmmakers at Godfather Films who make it possible to make a living doing what I love and to my good friend Alan Berg for his expert advice and assistance with publishing this book.

TABLE OF CONTENTS

CHAPTER 1

Do You Have Sand In Your Bags?

"Too many of us are not living our dreams because we are living our fears" **LES BROWN**

Picture a hot air balloon. Now imagine it's being dragged across the ground, violently bumping itself against rocks and hills. Now picture yourself in the basket of that balloon, going for a wild and scary ride. What are you going to do?

You could just jump out. You'd stand the risk of being injured in the fall and being stranded in the middle of nowhere, but you would probably survive.

But what if your original goal, when you climbed in the hot air balloon and fired up the gas burner, was to soar in the clouds, experience the adrenaline rush of flight and see things you had never seen before? What will you need to do to make this happen?

It's simple. You have to commit yourself to flight and empty the sand out of your bags.

Can you apply this principle to your own business? What is the sand in your bags that's keeping you from soaring? Is it a bad location, fear of learning social media skills, a bad web site, the wrong business partnership, an inability to network with others, close the sale, promote yourself or a lack of confidence in your product?

Let's face it, nobody is good at everything. It takes many skills to run a successful business and not everybody will make it. Many wedding professionals are really living job to job, dragging the ground like a hot air balloon full of sand in its bags. I want you to soar. Give yourself the credit you deserve. Look in the mirror and identify what you have to change in order to soar and then go make it happen.

In case you didn't already know… the sand is only a metaphor. Hot air balloons now use vents instead of sandbags. I didn't think it sounded as cool to say "Open the vent and let the hot air out of your life." It doesn't change my goal with this book, which is to provide you with valuable advice from the lessons I've learned, to help you and your business really succeed.

> *"Identify your problems but give your power and energy to solutions"* **TONY ROBBINS**

CHAPTER 2

―――

Puzzle Pieces

"Definiteness of purpose is the starting point of all achievement" **W. CLEMENT STONE** *– THE PAPERBOY WHO BECAME A BILLIONAIRE*

Have you ever put a puzzle together only to get to the end and find a key piece missing?

It just doesn't work and the value of your puzzle is now greatly diminished. You won't be able to sell the puzzle to anybody. Eventually you will lose all interest too.

Your business is just like a puzzle. You need all the pieces to make it work:

1. Quality Product – Today's clients are very educated and have a multitude of sources for similar products. We all need to do everything we can to be constantly improving our products and services. I've filmed more than 2500 weddings and have won tons of awards, but I still participate frequently in educational opportunities. The product I and my competition produce today is far greater than it was just a few years ago. If I had not improved my product, my competition would have taken all my business.

2. Marketing – Potential clients need to be able to locate you and vice versa. The tough part is that the best methods are in a state of constant change. Marketing strategies that worked great just a few years ago, such as Yellow Page ads and Direct Mail Postcards, have been eclipsed by social media. Did you know that Facebook advertising can be configured to display your wedding ads only to engaged women of a certain age in, a very small geographical area and you're only charged when they click on your ad?

3. Sales – Either your or your web site (preferably both) need to be good at closing a sales opportunity when presented. Learn how to identify your client's needs and/or wants, present an irresistible solution and then ask for the sale.

4. Business Plan – You need to know how you'll find customers and how much it will cost to produce your product. So many businesses are doomed because, even with a great product and lots of sales, there's no profit.

5. Tools – Abe Lincoln said "Give me six hours to chop down a tree and I will spend the first four sharpening the axe." You owe it to yourself and your clients to invest in dependable tools that WILL get the job done. I own an Audio Visual (A/V) Rental business... by accident. There's another company in my area that rents gear and I used them several times with varied results. The owner is a sharp guy but, while setting up for a job, there was a problem with one of the audio feeds. He jiggled the connector until it worked and said "it's been doing that for months". So we invested in our own A/V equipment, purchasing new gear as needed for bigger jobs as they came along. Before too long we had a substantial arsenal and the other company and others started renting from us.

6. Passion – There are so many ways to make a living in this world, I strongly encourage you to follow your passion.

> *"Most entrepreneurs are merely technicians with an entrepreneurial seizure. Most entrepreneurs fail because you are working IN your business rather than ON your business"* **MICHAEL GERBER, AUTHOR OF THE E-MYTH REVISITED**

CHAPTER 3

Keep It Real

"The best thing to hold onto in life is each other"
AUDREY HEPBURN

There's a reason why people get married, and it's not to ride in a limo, wear a new dress, look at photos or watch a wedding film. It's something much bigger and more special than any of the services you and I provide. We should all strive to make sure our couples enjoy their wedding experience.

This hit home for me while filming a wedding in the Caribbean. During the ceremony rehearsal, the couple was having a little difficulty understanding how they were supposed to respond to the questions the minister would ask during the ceremony. They were told by the minister to just remember to answer his three questions with one "I Will" and two "I Do's." I've filmed more than 2,500 weddings and usually I find the couple's vows and minister's message very personalized and inspiring. What a shame this couple would not be listening to the minister's message, rather they'd be trying to remember to count questions and respond with the proper phrase, so they wouldn't mess it up. At the end of the minister's instructions I pulled my couple aside and told them the answers to the questions are very easy. If the questions starts with "will you" the answer is "I will." If the question starts with "do you" the answer is "I do." They give a big sigh of relief realizing that now they could actually listen to what the minister was saying.

Many wedding professionals feel their contribution to a wedding is of prime important to its success. I would agree. If a bride wears a gown that makes her feel good, the whole day will feel better. If the entertainment is good, the party will be better. If a wedding planner handles all the details, the couples and family are free to better enjoy the event. If the meal is tasty, everybody is happy. Beautiful photographs and video will allow a couple to relive and share the fabulousness of the event. The list goes on.

But none of us are the most important. Everything we do for a wedding should honor the reason for the celebration. Two people publicly announcing their love and life goal of supporting each other for life. I tell my children that the ultimate goal in life is to be old and in love. We all smile when we see elderly couples hold hands, embrace or publicly express their love for one another. That's where we should all we want to be some day.

"Grow old with me! The best is yet to be."
ROBERT BROWNING

CHAPTER 4

What's In a Name?

"If your ship doesn't come in, swim out to meet it!"
JONATHAN WINTERS

When I started my film making business in 1984 I named it Cannon Video Productions, as a tribute to my father who was a radio disc jockey in the 1950's. His stage name was John Cannon. I liked the name and it served me well for a couple of decades. Then the internet, Google and texting became very popular and people no longer wrote anything on paper. Even when they know your name, they still turn to the internet to find you.

In the meantime, Canon cameras became very popular and more and more people were spelling my business name incorrectly as "Canon", instead of the way I spelled "Cannon." This wasn't such a big deal when people would look you up in a phone book, but it was disastrous once the internet became very popular. I ran into so many people who said they had tried to hire me but couldn't find me on the internet. To make matters worse, many of my referral sources had my company name and website address spelled incorrectly on their vendor referral lists. I was in big trouble.

I started buying localized, geo-specific domain names including RiversideVideo.com, RedlandsVideo.com, OrangeCountyVideo.com and many others. Eventually I had acquired 185 domains. Those provided great web traffic, but caused issues with my branding and identity efforts. We would try to give a domain and business name based on where the client was located. Sometimes we would give a client three different names within three different phone calls. At one time I had seven DBA's (doing-business-as another company name) all on the same checking account. The bank tellers would just roll their eyes when I made deposits. People couldn't remember our name and we had trouble remembering which name we gave them on our last job.

Traffic is only the beginning

Then I acquired WeddingVideo.com. It's a great domain which brings lots of traffic to my site. I also do a fair share of corporate video work for some very large companies. They weren't impressed that I film weddings and I got the feeling that most large companies wouldn't want to hire me, with a business name of WeddingVideo.com. While I was getting inquiries, and booking wedding business, I felt like I was crashing and burning with my business identity. I sought the help of a professional publicist and public relations (PR) firm.

We had a brain-storming session with the PR company to find a new name for the business. They said the first thing I should do is drop the phrase "video" and use the phrase "films." I agreed. I feel the word "video" means a recording whereas the word "film" communicates a story. Next, they said that since I was very well-known in the industry, I should make the new name of John Goolsby Films. Ta-dah… we're done. I sat and looked at them and finally said: "If people can't spell Cannon, they're never going to be able to spell Goolsby".

We kicked around ideas but weren't getting anywhere. Finally a young girl at the end of the table said: "I was Googling you and you come up all over the place. You've written a book, filmed more than 2000 weddings all over the world and you're in the Wedding Video Hall of Fame. You're like the Godfather of Video". I smiled and said "That's how they've been introducing me at conventions for years. I even own the domain TheGodfatherOfVideo.com".

The publicist said your new name is "Godfather Video by John Goolsby." I said we're not there yet. How about "Godfather Films"? Then we all smiled. We knew we had the right name. Then a realization hit us all simultaneously. What about the domain? If we can't get the dot com to match, we'll have to get a new name. Dot net and dot anything else just isn't the same.

It's the same with toll free numbers. As much as you tell people your phone number starts with 888 or 877, people will still hear, remember and dial the area code as 800. If you have a dot net or dot org, people will hear, remember and type dot com. I get lots of phone calls, emails and business intended for companies who have a dot net matching one of my 185 domains' dotcoms.

So we checked out www.GodfatherFilms.com and it wasn't available, but it wasn't being used either. The publicist had me try to track down the owner and acquire the domain. If that was unsuccessful, we'd have to start over. I agreed.

Let me make you an offer...

All domain owners have to register and unless they pay extra for privacy, it's very easy to find a domain owner's contact information. I found it, but it was all outdated. The phone and email no longer worked, but I had the owner's name. It took me a couple of days of research to find him. I told him who I was and how I wanted to use the domain. He didn't even know that he still owned it and thought it had expired. He told me I could have it for free! I told him I wanted to make it official and as he'd have to do some work online to complete the transfer, I told him I was going to pay him $100 for his trouble. He gave me his email and we closed the deal, via PayPal, while we were still on the phone.

That was a great investment! My domains used to get a very respectful 30 to 50 thousand hits per month. I got over 100,000 hits my first month with the new domain. It has since grown to more than 250,000 hits per month. I have literally booked jobs all over the world because of the great web presence. If you Google search "Godfather Films", we come up number one.

I was concerned about using the name legally since I knew of some pretty famous films and at least one well-known business with "Godfather" in the name. A quick internet search yielded hundreds of companies with "Godfather" in their name. I felt pretty safe using it in my new name.

You still have a long way to go after you find a great name for your business. I needed a new logo and the publicist gave us a few to choose from. None of them seemed quite right, so we decided to use a logo contest website, LogoTournament.com, to start an international logo contest. We ended up with hundreds from which to choose and ultimately paid a few hundred dollars for a great logo. There are several other online companies that follow the same contest model.

The publicist also created a brochure, that my in-house graphic artist re-designed, which has worked very well. For printing, we've used NextDayFlyers.com for great quality, pricing and quick delivery.

The most important element in your marketing these days is a great website and the most important part of a website is content. Without great search-engine friendly content your clients will never find you online. I did the basic design while one of my partners wrote all the code and applied good graphic design. We utilize a software program that allows us to customize the URLs (website addresses) for each of the 100+ client films we've uploaded to our site. That has been crucial to being found online. We frequently come up in searches above the venues and clients we feature in our various online films.

A major hotel and referral source called me saying they had just left a company board meeting where they were informed that I had hijacked their web site and now they have to get a dot net. I assured them that was not the case. They said they were all convinced it had happened because when they Google searched their hotel name and the word wedding, my web site came up ahead of theirs. I told them that part was true. My SEO (search engine optimization) outperforms their website, but I did not take their domain name.

While my company added its own flavor to the services the publicist provided for us, I am very grateful to them for knowing what needed to be done to rebrand and for walking us through the steps.

> *"Those who insert themselves into as many channels as possible look set to capture the most value. They'll be the richest, the most successful, the most connected, capable and influential among us. We're all publishers now, and the more we publish, the more valuable connections we'll make."* **PETE CASHMORE, FOUNDER OF MASHABLE**

CHAPTER 5

Today's Wedding Client

"A brand is no longer what we tell the consumer it is – it is what consumers tell each other it is."
SCOTT COOK, CO-FOUNDER, INTUIT

In years past, an engaged woman would attend a friend's wedding and, if impressed by the venue, catering, entertainment, flowers, etc., she would ask her recently married friend for referrals so she could use the same reputable sources for her wedding. Today's bride wants to be unique. She doesn't want her wedding to be anything like her friends'. The fact that somebody she knows got married at a particular venue is reason enough why she won't want to get married there. The same is true for entertainment and her other services.

I can remember working for groups of friends and where entire wedding parties were current or past clients. Those days are gone. Today's bride is on a mission to create an event that reflects her own individuality. She wants to plan a wedding that's unlike any she's attended. Today's bride is empowered by the internet to launch her own search for unique venues and vendors. These days if she doesn't find you online, odds are she won't find you at all. Not only do you need good search engine placement, you also need a site that speaks to your client and converts that traffic.

Being at the top of the first page of Google searches is critical. When doing a search only a small percentage of people go past the first page. I know I rarely do that and you probably don't either. The result at the top of the first page gets 100% more click-throughs then the second result on the same page. Subsequent pages get only a small fraction of that. Results number one and two will get more click-throughs than results three through twenty, combined.

How much should you invest in a good web site and Search Engine Optimization (SEO)? Quick answer: Enough, as compared to not enough. If you need an easy formula, determine the gross amount from your desired best sale in the upcoming year and invest at least that 2-3 times amount. I bet it will end up being one of your best investments of all time. Remember, it's not what it costs that matters most, it's how much you make. If your website isn't working... neither are you.

> *"All one needs is a computer, a network connection, and a bright spark of initiative and creativity to join the economy."* **DON TAPSCOTT**

CHAPTER 6

Who Wants Cheese?

"If you do not change, you can become extinct !"
SPENCER JOHNSON,
AUTHOR, WHO MOVED MY CHEESE

In 2002 I purchased an audio CD by Dr. Spencer Johnson, titled "Who Moved My Cheese?". I highly recommend the book. It totally changed the way I think about business. I don't want to ruin the story, but basically cheese is a metaphor for anything that is important to you, in my case, customers. You need to constantly increase the demand for your product, because unpredictable changes can occur with your current sources.

At the time I was running a successful business in Riverside, California. I was working out of an executive suite located one block from a hotel that hosted 400 weddings a year. I was filming 40-50 weddings a year as a sole proprietor. After listening to that great book, I promised myself that if a storefront ever became available next to the busy wedding dress store in our town, I would instantly lease it without debating my decision. My rationale was that a great way to increase demand for my business was to be seen by more brides. This wedding dress store was a landmark destination for the brides in our community.

The very next day after making this commitment to myself, I saw a banner on the building that read "Your Name Here". I walked into the 2,400 square feet space and instantly envisioned an Event Planning Showroom with lots of wedding vendors. I talked with the dress store owner who told me that it was a great location for her. She said that I should definitely rent it and she would send me tons of business. I leased the space on the spot, borrowed $50,000 against my house and built it out into a fabulous space. I then sub-leased space to photographers, disc jockeys, a florist, wedding planner, travel agent and limo company.

Eventually I also purchased the neighboring wedding dress store and turned that into a pretty good business, too. Within a couple of years my company was filming 250 events a year and we had over a million dollars in sales in 2005. I sold the dress store five years later for 6 ½ times my purchase price. None of this would have happened if I hadn't decided to take steps in order to avoid waking up one day wondering "Who Moved My Cheese?".

On average, more than 6,000 U.S. couples get engaged every day. Markets change and evolve. These 6,000 couples may not use the same methods to find their wedding vendors that yesterday's couples used. Therefore, we need to constantly be finding new methods to find our customers. Don't wait for the leads to dry up. Be proactive while things are good.

> *"Make your product easier to buy than your competition, or you will find your customers buying from them, not you"* **MARK CUBAN**

CHAPTER 7

Pricing Your Services

"The sting of poor quality lasts longer than the discomfort of high price" **NORDSTROM'S**

WEVA International (Wedding & Event Videographers International) hired me to speak on the subject of pricing at their convention in San Diego. Just before my program, I was approached in the lobby of the hotel by another videographer. He stated that he books 90% of the people who come to see him, so he must be doing everything right. Therefore he didn't think he needed to attend my presentation. I replied that if a high booking ratio was his only gauge for success, he should lower his prices even more. Then he'd book 100% of his appointments and, by his standard, be even more successful.

Can you say..."Sarcasm?"

My opinion is that anybody who has a booking ratio higher than 50% could charge more for their service or product. They're literally leaving money on the table. This is not about getting rich. It's about charging enough to deliver a quality product, provide you a good living and stay in business.

My dad built custom homes and used quite a few sub-contractors for various jobs such as framing, plumbing and electrical. He told me he always threw out the lowest bid, knowing that the subcontractor had probably underestimated the actual cost of doing the job and would cut corners or maybe even go out of business without finishing. Hiring the cheapest was a bad deal for everyone.

The number one reason consumers hire a professional is not cost, quality or selection. It's confidence. It's the belief that somebody can deliver what they promise. Confidence is defined on dictionary.com as "belief in the powers, trustworthiness, or reliability of a person or thing." A higher price in itself communicates an ability to deliver a higher-quality product.

I remember when I was a supermarket manager, at the young age of 22. My store was the chain's most profitable location on the west coast. This happened within 18 months of my promotion to manager, of what was previously a problem location. The main office was providing me with a lot of data that I don't think other managers really understood. To be honest, the chain really did nothing to train us. If we didn't perform, they just replaced us until they got someone who did. It was kind of like being self-employed, with nobody to really teach you. You had to learn it on your own. I spent a lot of time studying data to determine the most profitable items and those that had the least amount of labor requirements to stock. This was before computerized inventory control. I made an extra effort to ensure adequate stock of the most profitable and least perishable items. We were the most profitable store even before we had the highest sales. In store meetings I would tell my team that the overall sales number was all ego. It was the net profit that would provide us job security.

It's how much you keep

Many years later, while at a retreat for Top 25 International Filmmakers at my home, several of the very talented filmmakers were sharing information about the fees they were able to command. One of them made the statement: "It doesn't matter how much you make, it's how much you keep." And that's why pricing correctly and managing costs is so important. You should charge competitively enough to attract new business, but command high enough fees and manage your costs so you can make enough profit to stay in business.

While presenting a two day seminar in Minneapolis, back in the early 90's, a filmmaker in my class stated that there was no money in his town and nobody could locally charge the kind of fees I was getting. On a whim, I led the class outside and we stood near a busy intersection. I instructed them to count the number of luxury vehicles that passed us in just 15 minutes. We were all amazed at the high number. There was obviously plenty of money in his town, he just wasn't seeing it. I suggested that they adopt the philosophy that a high-quality movie of the biggest event in a person's life, is worth at least 6 monthly car payments.

Since that time I've had other students make similar comments about being unable to command higher fees in their market. I would ask them to name the nicest reception venues in their marketing area. If they named only budget brand hotels, I would tell them they were right... and that they should move to a better market.

It is very possible to successfully sell the same exact product with dramatically different pricing in the same local area. I was staying at the Waldorf Astoria Hotel in New York. There was a pop-up card listing the prices of items in the honor bar. A can of soda was $6.00. I looked out the window and saw a hot dog cart vendor on the corner. He was selling soda for $1.00 a can. He was directly in front of a convenience store that had a sign on the building advertising six packs of soda for 99 cents. I would venture to say that all three are successfully selling cans of soda with the hotel charging 36 times the price of the store next door.

Perceived value cannot be underestimated. Early on in my career I had three options on my brochure: Basic, Deluxe and Grand Deluxe. (I've since changed the names after I realized they all sounded like cheeseburgers.) They were priced at $590, $690 and $790. I read an article in the PPA Magazine (Professional Photographers of America) that recommended creating a very expensive, high-end package that would shock people with the price. It suggested that it would make it much easier to sell package number two.

So, I dramatically raised my prices to $790, $1290 and $1790 and distributed new flyers to the local wedding venues. A week later I received a call from a bride's mother stating that that a venue had referred me. She said that she wanted only the best for their daughter's wedding. She asked me to come to their home for an appointment. That was not my preference for meeting clients, but I agreed, mostly because I was struggling financially and this client sounded very promising. I even filled out an agreement in advance, for my new top package, and drove to their home.

Is anybody listening?

While I attempted to explain what came in my top package to the bride's mother, who did not seem very interested, the bride's father sat across the living room from us watching TV. She finally interrupted me and said the venue referred me, therefore I must be good, and she wanted to know the price of my top package.

As the amount was so much higher than I had been charging before, I couldn't bring myself to say the price out loud. So, I pointed to the price on the agreement indicating that she didn't have to pay the whole thing up front, she could give me a third as a deposit. She looked at the price and told her husband to "pay the man." He says "how much do I owe you?"

I stood up and walked across the room to Dad and pointed to the price again. He reaches into his wallet and pulled out a wad of hundred dollar bills and paid me in full. I started counting the money and was so nervous that I lost count... twice in a row. I wrote him a receipt marked "Paid in full".

I left and drove about a block from their house, pulled over and counted the money again, confirming it was all there. I remember thanking God for sending me this great job and the much-needed money. On the way home I stopped and paid a friend the money that I owed him.

I realized on that drive home that there were other customers out there, just like this, all the time. They had asked a referral source to recommend the best service providers. Venues often made their recommendation based on who was the most expensive. The client chose me because I was more expensive and took my most expensive package, not even knowing what was included.

Shortly after that a bride called asking the usual first question, "How much do you charge?". I offered to tell her a little about us and our quality and options and she cut me off saying "Just tell me your prices." I told her my recently raised prices and she said "thank goodness." She told me she had been on the phone all morning with other companies, getting very low prices, all under $1,000. She commented: "What can they possibly do for $1,000 that would be worth having?". She booked my top package over the phone! I can still remember the morning of her wedding, watching three limousines show up to transport her, her bridesmaids and her gown to the wedding. That's right, a limo for her, one for her bridesmaids and one for her dress. She also had me film her honeymoon in Hawaii. No kidding!

A bride's dad called and said he was referred to me by three different people and requested a meeting to discuss filming his daughter's wedding. I gave him my address and he said he was coming right over, with his family. After a couple of hours, when they hadn't arrived, I called and he said he had assumed we were professional, because of the many referrals, but he had changed his mind when he pulled up to a home address, rather than a business. He was of the opinion that you needed a storefront office to be professional.

Home may be where the heart is, but not the business

I attempted to debate this with him, but was not getting anywhere. The phone call ended on a sour note. I realized I could have felt the same way if I was on my way to visit a professional service provider such as a doctor, attorney or mechanic and they had not advised me, in advance, that I was meeting them at their home. I should have told this client in advance.

I called him back, apologized and asked for his permission to mail him a brochure, with a promise not to bother him again. He gave me his address and I sent the brochure. A few days later a check came in the mail for my top package. I was so happy to get the check that I didn't call and ask why he had changed his mind. I already had a bad phone conversation with him and didn't want to risk losing the job again. While filming the reception, the hotel catering manager approached me and told me she had heard about my encounter and knew why they had hired me. Dad told her that when he got my brochure, he told his family that anybody who charges prices that high has to be good at what they do.

If you want the best, you buy the best

I sensed that their life experiences had taught them that the more expensive options were usually the best value. I know that to be the case for many of my purchases, such as cars, clothing, attorneys, tax preparers and video equipment. And those clients were right. I did do a great job for them and their daughter's wedding.

Think about it. When is the best quality item, also the cheapest? Answer...Never. When is the highest price option the best quality?... Almost always, and usually also the best value in the long run.

I had purchased new windshield wiper blades for my truck which wore out very quickly. I went back to the store to replace them. The clerk asked if I wanted the blades for $4.99, $7.99 or $11.99. I did not take time to research online or even read the label. I told the clerk to give me the good ones. At about 2 ½ times the prices I anticipate the more expensive blades to last 10 times as long. I don't know if it's true, but that is my perception and I think it is common among consumers.

After consulting with various wedding professionals for almost three decades, reviewing businesses in all levels of success, I've decided that if I can only give a business one piece of advice, it would be to double their prices. Can I guarantee it will give you more success? Of course not. But I can tell you that, for the dozens of people I know who have followed that advice over the years, only one has told me it didn't work for them. And I have some reservations that they actually followed through. Most have told me that the perceived opposition to the higher prices didn't exist. They actually gained business or the reduction in volume was offset by increased revenue.

Can you do it?

I know that most of you will not follow this advice because you feel it's too risky. How about a risk-free formula for doubling your price in a year? Stay with me and modify the numbers to fit your business.

You could try using a capacity controlled pricing strategy similar to airlines and hotels. As the empty seats or hotel rooms begin to fill up, the prices increase. Let's say you are offering your product or service at 40 events a year, for $1,000 for each job, but you'd like to charge $2,000 for each job. Raise your prices now to $1,100 and raise them another $100 after every four bookings. By the time you reach your 40th booking, your prices will have doubled. If you double your prices and only book half the number of jobs, that wouldn't be a bad thing. You would have the same gross sales for half the work and re-duced operating costs. You'd actually make more profit.

What is the maximum you can charge for your product or service? I don't know and you probably don't know either. Your prospective clients do and they'll show you when they stop booking you as prices rise to a certain level. You can then roll your prices back to the price where you had the most success. If a competitor near you is charging more than you are, for the same service or product, then you should be able to raise your prices. Until someone tells you that you're too expen-sive, I will tell you that your prices are too low. A lot of new businesses decide to price their services or products a little lower than the price of existing businesses. What they don't know is that often the existing business is losing money and the new business will lose even more. Copy success, not failure.

Look at it this way

Here's another way to look at pricing. How much do you want to make? I'll use some easy numbers for this exercise. Modify them for your business as needed. Let's say you want to make $100,000 a year for your products or service while working 40 events per year. How much will it cost you to produce your product or service for those 40 events? You need to calculate your total costs, including all of your overhead expenses such as rent, vehicle payment, gas and mainte- nance, insurance, business license, advertising, material costs, payroll, tools and equipment (which have to be replaced before wearing out and failing on a job). Let's say you discover that it will cost you $5,000 a month to operate your business. Multiply that cost by 12 months ($60,000) and add it to your desired profit of $100,000. This means you need to have gross sales of $160,000. Divide that by the 40 jobs you want to do and you'll need to charge an average of $4,000 for each job you plan to do.

Over the years, I've used this exercise many times during consulta- tions. I wish I had been filming people's expressions when they realize that their business plans just won't work. I've run this same exercise with businesses charging $1,500 per job and watch it slowly sink in how far away they are from running a successful business. A lot of people in the wedding business work other jobs, or rely on their spouse's income to support their wedding business, which is really more of a hobby.

Treat it like a business

I've been the president of three different trade associations and in- volved with several more. I've received many desperate phone calls, over the years, from brides who never received their wedding gown, photos or video, or had their venue close without issuing refunds. I witnessed a couple of limo companies close between the time they took client's payments and the wedding, just weeks later. I've also had the sad duty of organizing fund raisers for the widows and families of wed- ding professionals who suddenly died, leaving their families literally penniless.

Spend some time determining how much it really costs you to produce your service and product. Determine exactly how much it's worth to your clients and how you'll find them. That's what it takes to be a successful business. All successful businesses know how to control their costs. Always be looking for ways to better manage your labor, utility, credit card processing, automobile and marketing costs. Lower cost options become available all the time. I've switched my workers comp, phone service and credit card processing services more than once, often at significant savings.

Cutting costs is only part of your success. If you want to keep more, you have to make more. Work on ways to ensure a steady stream of revenue. Running a profitable business is an obligation we have to our clients to ensure final delivery of a quality product.

> *"The superior man understands what is right; the inferior man understands what will sell"* **CONFUCIUS**

CHAPTER 8

Living in Harmony

"The most important single ingredient in the formula of
success is knowing how to get along with people"
THEODORE ROOSEVELT, U.S. PRESIDENT

Now I'm going to give you advice on a subject where I wish I was
much better... getting along with others. Much of the time we are on
the job in front of other referral sources and potential clients. If we
come across as a difficult team member, we can forget about future
jobs from any of those sources. When I say team member, I'm working
on the premise that most wedding parties and guests assume all wedding professionals at an event have all met and collaborated. They also
assume that we have the common objective of creating and document-
ing the best possible event for them, our clients. From their perspective
we are either a good team or a bad team... so let's be a good team.

I do have experience in this area. I was the president of Professional
Photographers of California. Try telling a wedding photographer they
can't stand in a certain area of the church, or that they have to limit
their supplemental lighting, or give them time limitations, or anything
else that impedes their artistic ability to create. Photographers are artists and one thing artists cannot stand is anything that restricts their
freedom, which in their mind limits their ability to be creative and
possibly disappoint their clients.

There's no "i" in Team

Whenever I show up on a job I want to be perceived as a team player.

I know that if I can do that successfully, I have a good chance at referrals for future work. I've got three techniques that have proven successful for me over the last three decades:

1. I'm not the smartest guy in the room I envision that everybody I encounter is smarter than me and knows the "Secrets to the Universe". It puts me in a mindset that makes me want to listen to everything people have to say. Nothing makes people feel more insignificant that not listening to them. I want everybody I meet to feel important.

2. Understand, then be Understood
When I arrive at a wedding job, before telling a photographer, banquet captain or wedding coordinator what I need from them, I make a point of understanding and delivering what they need from me. I'll ask photographers what angles they need for processional and ceremony shots. I'll find a way to work together so they get what they need. I find less resistance in making my requests with other professionals when I make a point of first understanding and accommodating their needs.

3. What can I do to make your life easier?
When I sense that another wedding professional is having a less than perfect day, I'll sometimes start our conversation by asking "What can I do to make your life easier?". Usually they just smile, but frequently they have a real answer, such as the photographer who forgot a tripod, or the church coordinator who needs help moving a heavy kneeling bench.

I've helped florists move flowers from the church to reception, because their truck broke down. I've poured champagne with catering staff when there was a mix-up in the timing of the toast. I've repositioned brides a few times during a bouquet toss, when I really didn't need to, as a subtle way of stalling while their photographer changed memory cards, lenses or batteries.

Nobody's perfect. You'll make mistakes. I suggest you own up to it when you do. It's worked out for me. Early in my career a wedding venue that was referring me asked me, at the last minute, to share an exhibit booth with them a local bridal show. I didn't really want to do that show as it was the next Sunday morning show and I had an all-day wedding the day before. But I wanted to stay on their vendor referral list, and in their good graces, so I agreed.

What goes around...

Here's where I made a mistake at that bridal show. I was grumpy from a lack of sleep and disappointed that the show was poorly attended by potential customers. Then the scheduled fashion show started, which pulled the few brides who did attend into the adjoining room. I went into the fashion show area holding a few of my brochures in my hand. The show promoter snapped at me not to put the brochures on the chairs and while I don't remember what I said, I know I snapped back in a very unprofessional manner.

A few weeks later a wealthy couple from my church called me from their vacation home in the Bahamas to ask about filming their 50th wedding anniversary celebration. We came to terms fairly quickly and I faxed an agreement to them. I called a week later since the agreement had not been returned. The client informed me that they had told their party planner about me and she told them she had a negative experience with me. The couple decided not to hire me. Their party planner was the same person I was rude to at that bridal show.

I called her office and they told me she was setting up a tent for a big wedding that weekend. I checked and we were both doing the same wedding. I drove to the location and apologized in person for the way I had acted at the bridal show. I said I was grumpy from lack of sleep but that didn't excuse my behavior. She replied that she was surprised because she had heard good reviews about me from several sources. I apologized again. She said it would never again be an issue between us and thanked me for my apology.

We got along great at the big wedding that weekend. That Monday afternoon I got a call from the clients in the Bahamas, booking me for their 50th anniversary. They had gotten a call from their party planner telling them they should hire me. Over the years, I've received corporate and event referrals, from that same party planner, worth more than $200,000. Best of all we've been great friends ever since. She even hired me to film her son's wedding. I now find it much easier to admit fault and apologize. You catch more flies with honey...

> *"Kind words can be short and easy to speak, but their echoes are truly endless"* - **MOTHER TERESA**

> *"Kindness is the language which the deaf can hear and the blind can see"* **MARK TWAIN**

CHAPTER 9

Most Improved Player

"Hire character, Train skill" **PETER SCHUTZ, CEO OF PORSCHE**

I loved playing basketball all through elementary school, junior high and high school. I wasn't as tall or talented as I wanted to be and was very sad when I realized I could never make the NBA. My only regret of skipping a year of high school and graduating as a junior was that I would also miss my senior year of playing hoops. In 1984 I was a supermarket manager, apartment manager and coached a basketball team for the local Boys Club. The team had some average talent, two exceptionally talented kids and then there was Fred (not his real name).

Fred impressed me to no end with how much effort he would put into his practices. Unfortunately Fred couldn't throw the ball as high as the rim or even bounce the ball very well. Scoring points is important in basketball and Fred wasn't going to be able to contribute in that category. But I loved this kid and his spirit and was determined to find a way to put his determination to use.

I would put Fred into games for a few minutes at a time and tell him whenever the other team had possession of the ball, I wanted him to go after that ball with everything he had. Fred would run, dive, yell, crash into referees, land upside down and anything else you can imagine. It was sometimes comical to watch and provided a lot of entertainment for those in the stands. It also intimidated the heck out of opposing teams. I would watch some kids just throw the ball and run when they saw Fred coming towards them. Fred never scored a point, but he led the league in steals and our team won the league championship.

You've should've seen Fred's face when we presented him with the "Most Improved Player" trophy. His parents were just as pleased. I'd like to think that the experience had an encouraging and lasting effect on Fred for the rest of his life. I
know it did for me.

For those of you with employees who might not have the skill or talent you'd like, but who have a good heart and work ethic, please think of this case study and how you can put your employee to work in a way that pays benefits for both of you. Highlight their skills and value, not their weaknesses.

"The coach is first of all a teacher" **JOHN WOODEN**

CHAPTER 10

What Do You Mean… What Do I Mean?

"Energy and persistence conquer all things"
BENJAMIN FRANKLIN

"You've got to say, I think that if I keep working at this and want it badly enough I can have it. It's called perseverance." **LEE IACOCCA**

Right after I opened my Event Planning Showroom, located right next to the busy wedding dress store, the so-called owner of the dress store disappeared. She had told me her business was doing great and she would be sending me lots of business. I borrowed fifty thousand dollars against my house and built-out this fabulous event planning showroom. I then sub-leased space to 10 other wedding professionals. I eventually learned that she was the managing partner and the business was not doing well. The IRS had already seized her checking account and she had simply walked away from the business. To this day, I don't know why she misled me about the success of her business.

The 10 vendors I had sub-leased space to all wanted the same thing I did, which was to be next to a busy wedding dress store. We all knew that the bridal gown is one of the first things a bride purchases, so the earlier we see a bride in the process, the better chance we have of a booking her. With the potential closing of the bridal store, I was at risk of losing my tenants and my $50,000 investment. I'm a confident guy, but I knew the other tenants did not lease space just to be next to me.

I began negotiating with the silent and sole remaining partner in the dress store. I eventually ended up purchasing the name and assets for a fairly good price, while also negotiating favorable terms with the landlord. We shared a common goal. Neither one of us wanted an empty space next to my showroom. Suddenly I was in the wedding dress business.How hard could it be? The reality is the wedding dress business may be one of the toughest in the industry.

I didn't know, what I didn't know... yet

As I quickly learned, there are over 150 gown manufacturers who showcase their products to retailers twice a year at trade shows called "The Market." I went to the market in Las Vegas, signed up for their workshops and started walking the aisles, trying to magically decide which gowns are going to sell and make me money. Turns out I do have good taste in this area (or lots of luck) and the first six lines I selected were popular lines. I told the manufacturer's representatives I would like to carry their line and they all responded "no."

WHAT? Why would they tell me no? I had a tough lesson to learn about retailing. Manufacturers protect their margins for retailers by limiting competition and the number of distribution points in a certain geographic area. Unless the lines have a good profit margin, retailers won't support the line. If too many retailers carry the line and saturate the market, there's so much competition between retailers that the profit margin erodes and it's no longer profitable to sell that product.

Dress manufacturers were telling me I couldn't carry the lines because they already had two in my city, or five in my county or ten in my state. In my discussions with other retailers I met at that market, I learned I had made good choices, but the manufacturers were going to be reluctant to let me carry a line because I was unknown to them. We survived the next six months with a couple of lines I was able to secure, either because the line was relatively new, or they were not as protective over the number of retailers.

I went back to the next Market, six months later, with a short film I produced about our business, along with a portable DVD player. I went booth to booth showing it to representatives and eventually secured the majority of the top lines I wanted. I was able to turn the dress store into a fairly successful enterprise. After owning the store for five years, I was able to sell it for six and half times what I paid for it. Talk about turning lemons into lemonade!

"How long should you try? Until." **JIM ROHN,**
MOTIVATIONAL SPEAKER AND FORMER CLIENT

CHAPTER 11

The Power of Networking

"Networking is by far the most important aspect of business school. The classroom is a distant second."
JAY DEVIVO, ENTREPRENEUR,
THE ANDERSON SCHOOL AT UCLA

A few years ago I received an email from an international wedding professional association, inviting wedding planners to sign up for three days of destination wedding training in Riviera Maya, Mexico. The part that really got my attention was that 240 destination wedding planners were expected to attend. Please don't think badly of me, but I registered for this event as a wedding planner and pretty much crashed the party.

My motivation was the fact that the economy was struggling. I had read that 20 percent of all U. S. wedding couples are having destination weddings and Mexico is their number one choice and I wanted a new source of business referrals. Upon arriving in Riviera Maya, the first thing I did was to introduce myself to the event management and fessed up to what I had done. I then offered to produce free promotional films for their event if they would let me hang out and network with the wedding planners.

They accepted my offer and immediately took me on stage and introduced me to everybody and how I would be filming the event. The wedding planners applauded my introduction and I made lots of great connections. Those contacts led to many great jobs, including a five-day destination wedding for 300 guests with a three-million dollar budget.

Hey, where's my listing?

Another international association was having their annual convention
in Southern California and I offered to film their event and promote
it online, in exchange for being listed in their program as the official
videographer. When I arrived and looked at the program, I didn't see
my listing. The president apologized and promised to make it up to
me. I expected to be introduced to the group, but that never happened.
I was feeling pretty depressed about the way things were going and
I might have been justified to walk off the job. I try to live my life as
ethically as I can and there is something about doing what you say you
will do, even when you feel others have not lived up to their end of the
bargain. I am so glad I stayed on that job. I got a call two weeks after
the convention appointing me to a regional leadership position. I met
and became friends with many wedding planners and one friendship
in particular has led to several great weddings and a few celebrity jobs.

I've also filmed several subsequent annual conventions and got my
listing in the program. This relationship has provided lots of benefits
to my career, including getting to know several genuine celebrities,
making friends all over the country and booking lots of great jobs, not
to mention the great education I've received.

While on a flight home from one of their conventions, I booked a
great job in Texas with the person sitting next to me on the plane. I've
served as president of three different trade associations and served on
various boards and committees. I've also spoken at more than 200 local groups along with state and international conventions.

Don't just join, participate

Something I frequently hear is that someone joined a group or association and they didn't get anything out of it. I can tell you from experience that your benefits will be limited if all you do is warm a seat at an
occasional meeting. It does take involvement in order to see benefit.
There are countless opportunities to get involved.

Some of the things you can do include:
- Helping set-up the room for meetings
- Serving as an officer
- Helping with raffles
- Photographing or filming their events
- Being a hospitality greeter

Some of the best jobs to have, if you want to meet everybody, are to volunteer to produce a newsletter, blog or to manage a Facebook Page. Your name will be in front of all members and frequently. You can also schedule meetings with prominent industry leaders and profile them in association publications. Everyone loves the publicity and it's also true that when you give to the group or association, without expecting anything, you'll always get back more in return.

Some of the benefits of trade association membership include improving your knowledge, skills and ability to do a good job for your clients. You'll enjoy access to some of the more influential people in the industry. Getting an appointment to meet with some of these people can be very difficult, especially if they've never heard of you. But being seated next to a celebrity event planner at an industry dinner can open many doors professionally. I've been added to many hotel vendor lists because of my contacts at trade association meetings.

You're only a stranger the first time

I know a lot of people feel uncomfortable making contact at events where everybody else seems to know everyone… except you. Don't be nervous. Everyone is there for the same reasons. They all want to expand their network with possible referral sources and get to know key people in the industry. Approach a few people and introduce yourself and then talk about everybody's favorite subject… themselves.

A strategy I use is to imagine two circles of information. One is everything there is to know about you and the other is everything there is to know about the person whom you are getting to know. If you visualize spinning those circles toward each other, they will eventually bump each other with the overlap being that piece of information you have in common. Maybe you both went to the same school, or have a common friend, or you recently worked at the same location or they manage a location that you really like. You may get an occasional cool greeting but my experience tells me that, more often than not, you'll make a new friend, a source of valuable industry knowledge and a potential referral sources for jobs.

Try to attend meetings outside your industry. If you're a disc jockey or photographer, attend the caterers meetings. If you're a florist or videographer, attend the wedding planner's meetings. You get the idea. Mingle with the people who could refer you. Attending industry asso-

ciation meetings may be the most affordable way to make the professional contacts that will build your business.

"Network continually - 85 percent of all jobs are filled
through contacts and personal references" -
BRIAN TRACY,
AUTHOR AND MOTIVATIONAL SPEAKER

"The richest people in the world look for and build
networks, everyone else looks for work"
ROBERT T. KIYOSAKI, ENTREPRENEUR AND AUTHOR

CHAPTER 12

My Three Life Lessons

"The two most important requirements for major success are: first, being in the right place at the right time, and second, doing something about it."
RAY KROC, CEO MCDONALDS

Life Lesson #1
It matters who you know. The right connections can open doors you can never reach.

I had several jobs before I was 16. I pushed a lawnmower around the neighborhood and mowed lawns, washed cars, delivered papers, worked in a deli and bicycle shop.

At age 16, it was time to follow the steps of my parents and three older brothers and get a job in a supermarket. I applied at a nearby store and was turned down three times in a row.

I went in a fourth time but this time with my mother who was grocery shopping. The manager turned me down again but saw me a few minutes later standing next to my mother in the check-out line.

He recognized my mother, probably because she was very beautiful but also a very good customer shopping for a family of nine.

The manager came over and asked me if she was my mother and I said yes. He rubbed his chin and said I could start Monday. My connection to my mom got me that job.

Life Lesson #2
There is a science to everything.

My first day on the supermarket job, the manager sent me to the produce aisle to mop the floor. He came by a few minutes later and told me I was doing it wrong. I know I must have given him a puzzled look wondering how somebody could mop wrong.

He then showed me which bucket was for clean water and which one was dirty. He showed me how to swing the mop for maximum coverage without splashing and how to apply the right amount of pressure to get the floor clean.

He was right. I was mopping wrong.

Life Lesson #3
Nobody can do Everything

During the 1970's while working in the supermarket bagging groceries, I noticed a customer in line as being somebody famous. He was Professor Julius Sumner Miller. I had seen him on the Art Linkletter Show and he was also the Disney Science Guy. He was a brilliant physicist who could explain how things work in a very entertaining way.

I said hello to him and told him I was honored to meet him. The cashier interrupted us to tell him he now owed $7.68 for his small order of groceries. He took all the money out of his pockets and laid it on the counter and looked up waiting for the cashier to count the money. I realized that one of the most brilliant minds of our time could not count money.

Nobody is the whole package and we need to accurately evaluate our own talents and abilities and either learn what we don't know or find somebody to do those elements where we just can't excel. Just because you are not talented in a certain area does not mean that you cannot be a fabulous success.

If one of those areas is bookkeeping or generating publicity for your company, you can always hire an accountant or publicist. If you choose wisely they will save or make you more money than you pay them.

"When you reach an obstacle, turn it into an opportunity. You have the choice. You can overcome and be a winner, or you can allow it to overcome you and be a loser. The choice is yours and yours alone. Refuse to throw in the towel. Go that extra mile that failures refuse to travel. It is far better to be exhausted from success than to be rested from failure." **MARY KAY ASH, FOUNDER OF MARY KAY COSMETICS**

CHAPTER 13

Living in the Lion's Den

"Keep your friends close and your enemies closer –
hopefully you will both stop being enemies"
JOHN GOOLSBY

When I started filming weddings in the 1980's, I could not find any sources of education on the subject. I reasoned that photographers have been in the wedding business for a while, why not just follow them and film whatever they shoot. Turns out photographers don't care for that much and most were fairly offish to me and rarely engaged me in conversation. One even turned to me during a post-ceremony photo-session I was filming and asked if what I was doing was "good video"? I know he wasn't saying it to be nice, but his words struck a chord with me and got me thinking.

At my next wedding, I decided to change my approach to wedding films. I said hello to the photographer at the beginning of the job and went to film the groom and groomsmen as he began photographing the bride and bridesmaids. Not only was I getting great stuff, like the guys fumbling with formal wear and making jokes about who the best man really was while drinking alcohol from hidden flasks, I wasn't impeding the photographer in his duties nor overwhelming my client with too many cameras at once.

When the photographer came in to photograph the guys, I went and filmed the girls and got a lot of natural un-posed emotional content for my client's wedding movie. The rest of the day went absolutely fabulous and the photographer approached me at the reception telling me how much he enjoyed working with me, mostly because he forgot I was there. He invited me to attend a gathering of "a group of local professionals who meet in our town once a month to discuss business matters". I really thought it was going to be something similar to an Amway meeting. Boy, was I wrong.

They like me... or do they?

It was the Inland Empire Professional Photographers Association meeting. I was standing at the back of the room as the meeting ended. The photographer who invited me approached with four other members. He said "John, this is our Board of Directors. Board of Directors, this is John. He does video and I like the way he works and I think he should be a member of our group. All in favor say aye". They all said "aye."

Then they just stared at me in silence. Then they started making comments:

> *"I did a wedding recently where the video guy wore jeans and a t-shirt and looked very unprofessional. I was so embarrassed because people thought he was with me."*

> *"I had a videographer put my proofs on video for the clients. That was stealing."*

> *"If I ever see another videographer put a tripod in the center of a church balcony again, I'm going to throw it off."*

> *"The video guy was filming me and I didn't sign a model release and I'm going to sue him."*

> *"I just call video guys vidiots."*

Bear in mind, this was at a time when wedding video was new and for the most part photographers really hated wedding videographers. So I was not totally surprised by their cold reception and I was happy some were actually talking to me. I didn't take their comments personally. After all, they didn't even know me. They were just expressing their perception of my industry. I thought I probably needed to change their perception of the video industry, or maybe actually change the industry, or more likely, both.

I went to their next meeting and a gifted photographer, named Merritt Smith, gave a very inspiring presentation. The program chairperson then stood up and announced that the following month was annual member month and one of the members needed to present a program. No one responded despite his endless begging for somebody to

volunteer. I was surprised to see my hand in the air since I had never spoken before a group, and this group hated everything about my chosen profession. After looking at me and emitting a long sigh, the chairperson asked "Anybody else...anybody?" "Okay, next month John will speak on... video."

In November 1988, I presented a program on how and why videographers and photographers should work together. I shared actual techniques and benefits that I had used and experienced. The program was very well received. Unbeknownst to me it was also election night for their Board of Directors. I was nominated from the floor and elected to the Board. Wow!

Is that the best you can do?

By joining the local group, I automatically became a member of Professional Photographers of California. They sent me a brochure for their annual convention which listed a single program on video production as part of their four-day event. I registered and paid for the entire convention, just to attend that single program and told several of my photographer friends that I was going.

It was not a good program. It was somebody showing home movies... and they weren't good. I met one of my colleagues in the hall following the seminar and he asked how I liked the video program. I unloaded about how bad it was. In a very calm voice, he said "Anybody can complain about the way things are, very few actually do something about it." Again, Wow! That was so profound. His statement both embarrassed and motivated me.

I sent a letter to Professional Photographers of California (PPC) thanking them for the great education and how I had learned so much from professional photographers about sales, marketing, composition and more. I encouraged them to invite more videographers to join their group so we can all learn from each other. I received a letter back appointing me Video Chairman. I flew at my own expense to their Board meeting in Sacramento. I spoke about my vision for encouraging more videographers to join their group to promote an atmosphere that facilitates harmony between the two groups. I also suggested hosting an annual PPC Video Fest.

I received another letter from them informing me that the nominating committee had put me on the ballot as treasurer. I ran for that office unopposed, but still worried about losing to write-in votes for anybody else. A lot of great things happened in my career by entering the so-called "Lion's Den".

Master Photographer, and life-long friend Carlos Lozano, saw me speak on the subject of Photographers and Videographers working together and hired me to teach a class at West Coast School. Wedding and Portrait Photographers International (WPPI) saw the listing and hired me to speak at their highly attended and respected convention... three times. The owner Steve Sheanin hired me to film his son's wedding, where I got to work side-by side with legendary photographers Monte Zucker and Clay Blackmore.

In with the In-Crowd

It was at WPPI in 1989 where I met Wedding and Event Videography Association (WEVA) founder Roy Chapman and I've been a featured speaker at all 22 of his WEVA EXPOs.

The year I was President of Inland Empire Professional Photographers (IEPP), our membership grew from 36 to 94 members. They also changed their name to Inland Empire Professional Photographers and Videographers (IEPPV). I claim to be the "V" in "IEPPV."

The year I was President of Professional Photographers of California our membership grew from just over 600 members to almost 800 members. I am now an honorary lifetime member.

I was invited to speak at the Professional Photographers of America Convention five consecutive years and earned Photographic Craftsman and Master of Electronic Imaging Degrees. I was appointed a National Print Juror and was offered a job as their West Coast Director of Membership.

These experiences have increased my business knowledge, my talent as a filmmaker and storyteller, enriched my life with great friendships with some very talented people and provided me with some great experiences all around the world. None of this would have happened had I not wanted to convert enemies to friends. I've discovered that adversarial relationship provide no real benefit in life for me, or for anyone for that matter!

> *"In the long history of humankind, those who learned to collaborate and improvise most effectively have prevailed."*
> **CHARLES DARWIN**

CHAPTER 14

Make It Legal

"Law and order exist for the purpose of establishing justice and when they fail in this purpose they become the dangerously structured dams that block the flow of social progress" **MARTIN LUTHER KING, JR.**

MAJOR DISCLAIMER: Business laws vary all across the world and change frequently. The purpose of this chapter is to expose you to the myriad of legal issues which most wedding professionals should be aware. My consulting experience tells me that so many of us do not understand all the things we need to do to protect our businesses legally and financially. Please consider this chapter a vehicle to create awareness and never act on legal advice from anybody who is not a fully qualified legal professional. I am not that person. The information shared in this book is for informational purposes only and not for the purpose of providing legal advice. You should contact your attorney to obtain advice with respect to any particular issue or problem.

There are many legal aspects that small business owners must follow. Violating a government policy on how we are supposed to run our business, collect and report sales tax and compensate our employees and/or subcontractors can have serious financial consequences. Laws and legal codes, along with the varied interpretations of them, will vary from state to state and city to city. I strongly encourage you to seek out competent legal advice on how to structure your business and report your income. I consulted with an experienced certified public accountant who gave me great advice. I am not a lawyer or accountant, so the following is just to give you basic information to get you thinking. Please consult an experienced lawyer and accountant before choosing which business structure is right for you.

Business Structure

Sole Proprietor is the most common structure for small businesses. It is the easiest and least expensive to set-up. It will mean one owner for the business who will file one tax return for personal and business income. It is owned and run by one individual and there is no legal difference between the owner and the business. Due to having unlimited personal liability, they are generally not for people with significant assets. If someone sues your business, they could end up owning your business along with your personal possessions. Sole Proprietorships are easy to create and also, very easy to dissolve.

It is still the structure I recommend for most small business owners who are without a lot of assets. You'll need a great contract that limits liability and insurance to protect yourself from lawsuits and other losses. Think of it like car insurance. If you have no assets you really only need to purchase the bare minimum coverage. People are unlikely to invest the money to sue someone who has no ability to pay. People with significant assets are targets for lawsuits and may need to purchase additional liability insurance to protect themselves.

Creating a Corporation is often the choice for individuals with significant assets, since generally your personal assets are not at risk should the business fail or be sued. You'll need to have a state charter that classifies your business as a separate entity and it will experience more regulations, paperwork and fees (again, please consult qualified legal experts for this). Shareholder dividends are not deductible which can result in more overall taxes being paid. A corporation is an organization that is created with specific state laws as a separate entity from the shareholders. An important feature of a corporation is limited liability. If a corporation fails, shareholders may lose their investments, and employees may lose their jobs, but neither will be liable for debts to the corporation's creditors.

Limited Liability Companies (LLC) are a hybrid and available in most states. Typically it will have managing partners whom will have limited liability. When setting up the LLC, you may be able to allocate profit and loss between the business and personal income and choose whether to be taxed as a partnership or a corporation.

They are similar to corporations because personal liability is limited and similar to sole proprietorships because of the availability of pass through income taxation. It is usually more flexible than a corporation, and works well for companies with a single owner.

Business License

Most cities and/or counties will require you to obtain and display a business license and pay a fee based on a number of factors, usually the estimated annual sales and/or the number of employees. Frequently, downtown areas will add assessments to the cost and use those fees for marketing purposes. Business licenses are not usually expensive, but being caught without one may incur financial penalties.

Contracts - Agreements

To protect you and your clients, you should have a written agreement for each job. Since most clients meet with many service providers and we all meet with a lot of clients, it would be easy for somebody to not understand or remember incorrectly the terms of each agreement. Putting agreements in writing helps prevent misunderstandings later.

In order to be an enforceable agreement, it needs to specify the services and/or products provided along with dates, times and locations where the job(s) will take place. You need to spell out the payment schedule and a cancellation and refund policy. Even if your policy is no refunds ever, it still needs to be in writing.

I encourage including a model release and not just for photographers and filmmakers. Wedding planners, florists, DJ's and others will occasionally want to use promotional photos and video from events in ads and web sites.

Since many of us cover a fairly large geographic area, specifying a local jurisdiction for disputes could prevent you from traveling a long distance for multiple court dates. Specifying arbitration as the method to settle disputes may prevent you from having to pay large legal bills.

Many contracts will also include a meal and break policy and consider using the phrase "non-refundable retainer" for the initial deposit. I have always included a clause limiting my liability, for any and all reasons, to the fee charged.

Since this document is one of the most important you will use in your business, I suggest having a local legal expert who knows the courts in your area and how judges typically rule on similar matters, review your contract.

Property Tax

Many businesses are unaware that many counties require you to report and pay property tax on your business equipment. Again, failure to report and pay will incur penalties.

Taxable Sales

This one of the most misunderstood areas for small businesses and the one that potentially introduces a huge risk. Most states require businesses to collect sales tax on most products and many services, report and forward those taxes to the state on either a monthly or quarterly basis. Failure to collect required taxes will expose you to potential penalties. Make a point to find out exactly what is required in your state and follow the law to the letter. You may not be required by your state to collect sales tax when the job is performed and the final product delivered outside of your state. The state in which you do the job will have their own set of rules that may require your client to report the purchase and pay the sales tax directly to the state. Please be sure to check with the state taxation bureaus and your financial advisor.

Purchases

If you make a purchase at a local store, the retailer will collect the proper sales tax from you and forward it to the state. If you make your purchase online, the retailer may or not collect sales tax from you. Odds are your state requires you to report the purchase and pay the appropriate sales tax directly to the state.

And now a tip for my fellow filmmakers in California – If you purchase post-production equipment in California and supply the retailer with a Section 6378 Exemption Certificate, you may not have to pay the state portion of the sales tax. You may still have to pay any county or local city tax, but you may save 5 to 7 percent on your purchase.

Office Space

If you decide to rent commercial space for your business, you will want to negotiate the best possible terms. Landlords hate empty space. They're not making any money and will find it hard to rent adjoining space if the location is full of empty spaces. Nobody wants to rent in a ghost town. They'll often give rent concessions and agree to improvements for longer term leases. That means you can ask for new carpets, paint and offices built to your design in exchange for a long term lease.

Going month-to-month incurs the least amount of risk of being on the hook for a long period of time if your business should fail. It does have the risk of the landlord raising the rent at any time. It could even double or triple which could be devastating.

If you are fairly comfortable that you will be in business for a long time, in the same geographic area, try negotiating a longer term lease, maybe two or three years, for a fixed rate each month. You can even ask for options to renew three years at a time for the same rate. Best case scenario is you get a great lease for three years with options to renew at the same rate for three more three year terms.

Beware of the "Triple Net". A triple net lease is where the lessee agrees to pay all real estate taxes, building insurance, and maintenance costs, in addition to the rent. While they are common, I have never paid them. Many landlords who include this in the agreement will provide the tenant with a bill at the end of the year. And it could be a huge shocker of a bill. It could include all property tax, water and trash bills, insurance and repair bills for the entire complex and divided by the square footage of each tenant. Sometimes there is no documentation for the individual costs, just a huge bill that you are expected to pay. Maybe the building needed a new roof, AC units or a repaving of the parking lot. I'm not saying it isn't fair to arrange such an agreement, I'm just saying that, personally, I don't like the risk and surprise of huge bill for an unknown amount. I prefer to pay a set rate each month and that is what I have always negotiated. Your best bet is to consult a real estate professional and attorney to see what's best for you.

Insurance

More and more venues are requiring vendors to provide proof of Liability Insurance before you can work on their property. I think that it's a good idea for the property and the vendor, for both of your protection. When something unfortunate happens, everybody gets sued. Common minimums include $1 Million per occurrence and $2 Million aggregate. Included in the same policy may be equipment insurance, in case of loss, fire or theft. There have been many reports of well-dressed thieves who hang out at wedding venues and just wait for you to turn your head while they and your gear disappear. I use Think Tank camera bags which have security cables and built-in locks. I can always find a gift table or stage support to secure my gear. When I travel, I find something within my hotel room to secure my gear.

Check your policies to confirm you are covered when you travel out of state and/or country. I once had an agent tell me I was covered world-wide but when I did a closer read of the policy, I discovered he had made an error. Consult with a reputable insurance professional for your options and costs. Also check what the minimum requirements are for the venues where you work.

While liability insurance covers injuries and accidents, think of Errors and Omissions Coverage as professional liability insurance. It will cover things like your failure to show up for an event, lost files, making a mistake on your calendar, etc.

Workers Compensation Insurance is mandatory for most employers and penalties for failure to provide it are substantial. I was originally paying fairly high premiums but found out I could save about half of what I was paying by getting it through my online payroll service, Intuit. I also now pay a fraction in payroll administration compared to what I was paying to a very popular payroll service. I simply enter my employee's hours to Intuit's website and print my employee's checks on my printer. It will also do automatic payroll deposits. It keeps track of payroll taxes and forms and make and files those on time. Did I mention it saves me a ton of money over the typical payroll service? Consult your accounting and tax professional to see what the right solution is for you.

As your business grows you'll want to bring on help. There may be incentives for you to use independent contractors,over employees, such as saving money on payroll service, unemployment insurance and payroll taxes. They are usually only considered independent contractors if they provide their own tools, choose their own hours and if they work for multiple clients. Employees usually have tools provided by the employer as well as having to work hours designated by the employer.

Check out IRS SS-8 to help you decide in your particular situation. Having the IRS reclassify one of your subcontractors as an employee will be a huge financial hit. If you use independent contractors, you need to check and see if your insurance policies cover them while they are working for you. If not, have your independent contractor provide their own proof of insurance. Remember, it's not just how much you make, it's how much you keep. Inadequate coverage could mean you lose it all because of some unfortunate accident.

As with everything else in this chapter, please consult qualified legal, financial, real estate and tax professionals to get the right information for your business and area.

"Give to Caesar what is Caesar's and to God what is God's" **JESUS OF NAZARETH**

CHAPTER 15

Elevator Speech

"...Paint generously and unhesitatingly, for it is best not to lose the first impression." **CAMILLE PISSARRO**

How often do we meet someone in passing, where you know you only have seconds to communicate to them the services or products you have to offer? Forget trying to make a long speech, they're not that interested, yet. You have maybe 30 seconds to make that first impression.

These are called Elevator Speeches. You should have one...here is mine:

"Since the beginning of recorded history, the wedding celebration has been the most important event of our lives. All the most important people on the planet to you will be in one place, at one time. The challenge is that all memories fade and most will eventually disappear. I produce a product that will allow you to give your grandchildren the most incredible gift of all time. They will be able to introduce your grandparents to their grandchildren. My name is John Goolsby and I sell time travel".

Maybe it worked or didn't work for you, but I've had people cry upon hearing it.

Once we get past my elevator speech the conversation can go in any direction. It may be that their biggest regret is that they didn't have their wedding filmed, or they have a friend getting married or how they wish their sister had hired me or how they hadn't thought of having their wedding filmed, until now. So far, it has always been a good conversation starter for me. From there I usually progress to showing samples on my iPhone. I've booked four really good jobs while on airplanes.

Telling someone what you can do for them in 30 seconds, or less, is a lot harder than it sounds. You have to be ready to say your Elevator Speech without warning. That's why I recommend practicing it, out loud, as often as you can. That way you'll be well rehearsed for when you get to really use it, such as at a networking event, or online at the grocery store.

I can guarantee that whatever elevator speech you start with and try, you'll learn what works and what doesn't and, over time, it will evolve into something really good. You know we're all impressed by the pyramids and marvel at the precision of the architecture. However, the first pyramids weren't so perfect. They were actually very poorly constructed. We learn from our mistakes... it's called experience.

I can remember telling my kids: "Experience is what you get when you didn't get what you wanted". Early in his career, my son would come home after a job and tell me: "Dad, I got some more experience today". I knew it meant something had gone wrong, but he had learned a valuable lesson and would do better on future jobs.

> *"The only source of knowledge is experience"*
> **ALBERT EINSTEIN**

CHAPTER 16

Marketing with Legs

"Many a small thing has been made large by the right kind of advertising" **- MARK TWAIN**

Being the treasurer of Professional Photographers of California (PPC) for four years was a great learning experience. One of my duties was to secure sponsorship for various events. One time, a potential sponsor told me he was in, but he needed "marketing with legs". How's that again? He then told me that the last event he sponsored was a "Moon Pie and Dr. Pepper Party" at a photographer's convention in Atlanta. He felt that if participants had a good time at the party and knew his company had sponsored the event, for the following months they would think of his product every time they had a Moon Pie or Dr. Pepper. Instead of a single impression for his advertising dollars, he wanted a way to be remembered past the sponsored event. I knew right then that I wanted marketing with legs, too.

That was where I got the idea to start handing out branded coffee cups to the hundreds of wedding professionals who were in a position to refer me. These handsome black mugs have my gold logo on one side and the phrase "I'm the expert… Shut up and write the check!" on the other side. People always laugh when I hand them out, knowing it's a comical way to promote my business and provide a dose of self-motivation as people drink their morning coffee.

I've had dozens of people tell me they drink out of my coffee cup every day. For roughly $3 a piece, I have a marketing piece that puts my name in front of a referral source every day of the year, for less than a penny a day.

"Give your event legs" is one of my closing phrases to sell corporate same-day edits. A same-day edit is where we edit a highlight film of an event, while it's happening, and then premiere and distribute the film at the conclusion of the event. Attendees take the film with them when they leave, to have it to share with family and colleagues. I tell my clients that, since they invested a lot of money to impress or motivate clients or employees, it would be a nice touch if when the event ends, it really isn't over. I can give their event legs and a life well past its usual end point. I've been able to book these jobs all across North America.

Make it social

I cannot understate the importance that social media plays in the jobs my business receives. There are a lot of choices out there for what I do and it exceeds the current demand. I wanted to find a way to stay in front of my 4,000+ Facebook friends on a regular basis. Since I travel quite a bit, I have the opportunity to post pictures from my jobs around the world. Every week I'll post photos and ask my friends "Where in the World is Godfather Films?" The first correct and/or most entertaining answers receive a Starbucks Gift Card from me which is custom printed by Starbucks with my logo. Some of my posts have had thousands of views.

I've shared my successes in order to motivate you to create your own original "Marketing with Legs" ideas. Please don't copy mine. Rather find a way to make it your own. Some of you are probably wondering how to use Facebook to build business. Facebook is a great way to create an awareness of your own brand. We film Same-Day Edits at weddings and post them on Facebook the night of the wedding. We tag the Bride and Groom in the film. We then use the names in their wedding program to tag as many of the wedding party and vendors as we can.

And she tells two friends...

We have over 4,000 Facebook friends. Most of our clients have 200-500 friends. Each of their friends has just as many friends. Every time someone leaves a comment on one of our Facebook films, all of their friends can be exposed to our work. Thousands can see our work within days. We send a message to our couple's encouraging them to tag their wedding party and guests (since you can only tag people you're friends with on Facebook). I had a bride email me, during her tropical honeymoon in Tahiti, from her hut over the water, asking me how to tag friends on her wedding film that we had uploaded to Facebook. We sent her instructions and she emailed me an hour later saying she'd reached her maximum number of tags. We didn't even know there was a maximum. Did I mention she was on her honeymoon! Brides love sharing their weddings and encouraging them to use their wedding film to make that happen, gets our name in front of thousands every year.

Did you know that fifty percent of an average wedding party is engaged or will be within three years? I want all of these people to know about Godfather Films. I almost forgot… please like me at www. Facebook.com/GodfatherFilms

"Learn from yesterday, live for today, hope for tomorrow."
ALBERT EINSTEIN

About the Author

JOHN GOOLSBY, *MEI, CPV, MPV, Professional Storyteller*

John Goolsby is an award winning filmmaker, author, convention speaker, college professor, property manager, business coach and the recipient of the Bob LeBar Vision Award for Innovation and Entrepreneurial Spirit. He's a 27-year veteran of the wedding and event industry, having filmed more than 2,500 weddings, in 23 states and 12 countries. Actors, Rock Stars and Professional Athletes have commissioned him to film events around the world, some with multi-million dollar budgets. His corporate client list includes Abbott Labs, Kaiser Permanente, Costco, Penske Motorsports, Mobil Oil, B. F. Goodrich, U. S. Foodservice and the U. S. Army

He's the author of The Business of Wedding & Special Event Videography, which received Four Stars from Videomaker Magazine and was chosen as Popular Photography's Book of the Month. It is required reading for those seeking Merited Professional Videographer status from the Wedding and Event Videographers Association (WEVA).

Business Coaching for Wedding Professionals is just one of his specialties, having presented more than 200 seminars and workshops. His audiences include industry trade associations such as Association of Bridal Consultants (ABC), Association for Wedding Professionals International (AFWPI), National Association of Catering Executives (NACE), Professional Photographers of California (PPC), twice for Show Biz Expo, three times for Wedding & Portrait Photographers International (WPPI), five times for the Professional Photographers of America (PPA), Wedding MBA (Merchant Business Academy) and a record setting 22 consecutive years for WEVA (Wedding & Event Videographers Association).

rofessional Trade Associations have honored him with leadership positions
ncluding being the California and Nevada State Coordinator for the Associa-
on of Bridal Consultants (ABC) and the President of the Professional Photogra-
hers of California (PPC). He is an Honorary Lifetime Member of the New York
rofessional Videographers (NYPV) and Professional Photographers of California
PPC).

Iis honors and awards include an induction into the Wedding Video Hall of
ame, 3 Telly Awards, 7 Creative Excellence Awards, The Trendsetter Award –
)range County Association of Bridal Consultants, The Communicator Award,
he Videographer Award of Distinction, Best Production under $30,000 – Na-
ional Association of Catering Executives (NACE), 8 AAA Artistic Achievement
Awards, ANNE Award – 1st place Web Design - Professional Photographers of
America,PROVA Award – Best Wedding Video in United States – Three Years in
Row, Proclaim Award– Best Video Fund Raising, U.S. Catholic Church

ohn's Professional Designations include:

Certified Destination Wedding Specialist –
    Mexico Tourism Board
Certified Professional Videographer –
    Association of Professional Videographers
Merited Professional Videographer –
    Wedding & Event Videographers Association
Master of Electronic Imaging and Photographic Craftsman - Professional
    Photographers of America
Voted One of the Top 25 Event Filmmakers in the World three years in a row by
    the readers of Event DV Magazine.

'or more information about John's services and how he can help capture and
roduce a wedding or event film for you or your client,
mail John@GodfatherFilms.com, visit www.GodfatherFilms.com,
r call 800-495-5530

Acknowledgements

"John Goolsby is a legend in the wedding industry and has set an example by not only rebranding his business for the future, but now sharing his knowledge and secrets for success with other wedding pros, new and experienced. This book is a must-read for anyone in the wedding industry who is looking to take their business to greater heights."

ALAN BERG, PROFESSIONAL SPEAKER - AUTHOR - MARKETING GURU
ALANBERG.COM

"Full of wisdom & valuable insights. I think John is one of the smartest guys in the wedding business. I learn something new every time we talk."

DJ DR. DRAX, PRESIDENT
AMERICAN DISC JOCKEY ASSOCIATION

"John Goolsby is a wedding industry presenter who speaks from direct experience. In his role as a professional wedding filmmaker, John has developed a 360-degree awareness of weddings and receptions. It is that skill which makes him a master collaborator with fellow wedding professionals and fueled the authoring of this book. We're left with just one question. When can we look forward to Volume 2?"

ANDY EBON, SPEAKER - WRITER - CONSULTANT
THEWEDDINGMARKETINGBLOG.COM

"John is a respected leader within the industry and we have been fortunate to have him speak at the Wedding MBA Convention five times. He has helped thousands of wedding professionals with his knowledge and sage advice. We had him document our daughter's wedding. His same-day edit video was the perfect cap to the reception!"

WILL HEGARTY, CHANCELLOR
WEDDING MERCHANTS BUSINESS ACADEMY

"John is a master at his craft. His work for ABC has been fabulous and we highly recommend that others learn from him."

DAVID M. WOOD, PRESIDENT
ASSOCIATION OF BRIDAL CONSULTANTS - ABC

"When designing one of the most technical and over the top weddings of my career, I knew I had to fly in John Goolsby to film it."

FRANK J. ANDONOPLAS, MBC
EVENT PLANNER OF THE YEAR, EVENT SOLUTIONS
ONE OF THE TOP TEN BRIDAL CONSULTANTS IN THE COUNTRY,
ASSOCIATION OF BRIDAL CONSULTANTS

"John has an extraordinary sense of beauty, movement and storytelling that captures dreams in action! But it is John's professionalism and commitment to assisting others along their journey that keep clients and vendors coming back for more of "Godfather Films"! John and his team are the best of the best!"

MARY DANN, OWNER
MARY DANN WEDDING AND PARTY COORDINATORS
CELEBRITY WEDDING PLANNER & HOST OF
"WHOSE WEDDING IS IT ANYWAY" & "PLATINUM WEDDINGS"

"Most people have a dream and they either make it or they don't. With the hit the economy took a few years ago I saw many companies say goodbye to their dreams. John Goolsby, however, chose to refocus his direction. With his new awareness John has completed the re-branding of his company and I cannot wait to read his book! I hope you will have the same eager anticipation."

RICHARD MARKEL, PRESIDENT
ASSOCIATION FOR WEDDING PROFESSIONALS INTERNATIONAL, AFWPI

"John's book is written with insight from his personal experiences as a creative professional and business owner. The writing style is informal and direct. His success comes from listening, observing, interpreting and applying. An excellent blue-print for success for all business owners in any category. This inspiring digest is useful for newcomers in the industry, as well as a refresher for all of us already well-established. It will be in my personal library as well as on my list of gifts of appreciation and inspiration when the occasion calls for it."

RENÉE STRAUSS, INTERNATIONAL BRIDAL SYLIST
FOUNDER OF RENÉE STRAUSS FOR THE PLATINUM BRIDE
STAR OF TLC'S BRIDES OF BEVERLY HILLS

Made in the USA
Las Vegas, NV
26 September 2025

28632874R00038